# *Qualifying*

# *And*

# *Closing*

Part Two

SALES TRAINING

Wayne E Shillum – Author

WES MARKETING

# QUALIFYING AND CLOSING

Wayne E Shillum - Author

WES Marketing

# DEDICATION

This part is dedicated to the many dead ends I pursued
And to the many people, I made presentations to
That had no need, no interest or no money
to purchase my offerings

**Before I learned**
**How to Qualify Prospects**
**And ask the right Closing Questions**

It is also dedicated to the many information sources
That got me on the Right pathway
My number one mentor was my Father - R H Shillum

**Other Mentors Were**

J Douglas Edwards - Earl Nightingale

Dale Carnegie – Napoleon Hill – W Clement Stone

Norman Vincent Peale

And the many others who provided the Inspiration

And knowledge for my Career

Table of Contents

# INTRODUCTION

## QUALIFYING IS THE FIRST PART OF

## THE SELLING PROCESS

THE SELLING PROCESS is a journey that involves creating the complete transformation of a stranger or potential prospect into a buying customer.

Your selling process begins with the qualification of the client's needs and their willingness to genuinely consider your offerings.

The qualifying continues with the verification of their interest throughout the entire journey and reaffirming your accuracy in providing the solutions to meet their needs.

**It is also Confirming that they meet your Company's Needs**

**Closing** is not just something that comes at the end of your efforts. It is a planned course of action structured to reach a positive result, which is "the completion of the sale."

The common references that are made to "Closing the Sale" will usually describe it as the point in time; when you are in front of the prospect, at the end of your sales presentation, and you are asking for the order.

**Not Completely True**

The Close is not just a point to be reached. It does not come only at the end of your sales presentation. "Closing the sale" is the journey you take to reach the final confirmation of your efforts.

**Both Qualifying and Closing**

**Allow you to Accomplish the Selling Process**

### The Beginning

You should be shaping your final close right from the minute you open your mouth and the first time you contact or talk to your prospect.

1. The process starts with establishing that there is a need and interest in your products or services (offerings).

2. You will then learn how the client will benefit from your offerings through meeting(s), before your final presentation.
3. At the end of your final presentation, you will ask for the order and Answer any Questions to secure it.

Whenever you ask a closing question, you will often get a question or objection to placing the order with you.

Closing and Overcoming Objections are a team. We call them the "Dynamic Duo"). We will cover them in two separate parts of our training for clarity sake. *(Overcoming Sales Objections is Part Three.)*

Some people may think that teaching the skill sets of Closing and Overcoming Objections this early in the sales training, is out of sequence.

Yes, prospecting or finding clients is usually what you will do first in your sales efforts. Holding introductory and fact-finding Meetings is also an activity early in the process.

However; the knowledge of Closing and Overcoming Objections are essential skill sets that are required before you are able do anything else in the selling process.

**They Will Be Needed**

- As soon as you start prospecting
- When you contact your first prospect
- During your introductory and fact-finding meetings
- In your final presentations.

# Qualifying, Pre-Closes, Final-Closes

There are many ways to qualify, pre-close and make your final closing attempts.

You should know as many closes or closing questions as possible, because each situation will be a little different.

1. **Qualifying** a prospect is achieved by asking closing questions.
2. **Pre-Closing** questions are also needed to confirm that you are moving in the right direction in your information gathering meetings and during your final presentations.
3. **Final Closing** – These attempts should get the order.

The Prospect's Answers will show if your efforts are successful

There will be similarities to many closing attempts. With knowledge and practice, you will be able to select the right qualifying questions or closing method.

Memorizing the sample questions or the closes that we will be providing, does not mean you will need to recite them verbatim.

The secret is to learn them, understand how they work, and why they work; so, you can put them into your own words and everyday use.

- The closing process must become you
- Not a robot that is repeating someone else's words verbatim.

**What the Qualifying and Closing Process Involves**

It Determines if you have a real potential client by:

1) Establishing Needs
2) Finding Solutions
3) Creating Interest and Desire to Purchase
4) Having a Compelling "Call to Action"
5) Getting the Order when you are done
6) Staying on course during the entire process

## The Closing Process

### 1)Qualifying

In Part One, we outlined the key elements that need to be present in a prospect. Qualifying verifies that these elements are there. Qualifying is essential, and it is the first part of the closing process.

Qualifying establishes a prospect's needs, their willingness to consider your offerings, and the desire and ability to pay.

It is better to miss one potential client by over qualification than waste time with 10 or 15 who have no potential.

The best part about taking this qualifying approach is; that if you feel afterward that you have missed a good potential client in the process, you can always call them back and have a second chance.

In the meantime, you have saved a lot of time by removing prospects with no potential. Not everyone will become a customer!

### 2)Pre-Closing

When you make your follow-up calls; to gather more information for your sales presentations, you should also be asking questions that further shape your final close.

Too many sales people visit the prospect and tell them what they are selling and try to convince the client to purchase their offerings without finding out if their offerings will meet the prospects needs.

**They Spend Too Much Time Telling**

**Not Enough Time Asking and Listening**

The goal of a sales person is to discover where they can help their prospect achieve what they are looking for.

You must show the prospect that your mission is the same mission as theirs.

This mission is to find a solution to any problem they have or meet any requirements that they have and provide the benefits of your offerings in the process.

### The Procrastinators

The questions that you will ask during your initial meetings are all mini closes to determine if the prospect has a need, any interest in trying your offerings (and often missed, the intent to buy or ability to pay.)

The procrastinating sales people who wait until the end to ask any qualifying or closing questions will waste a lot of time. They are often so afraid of hearing a NO, that they will postpone any attempt that will Create one.

They rush through their presentation covering all their features and benefits without giving the prospect a chance to say anything.

They are then surprised when the prospect thanks them for coming and says they do not have a need and are not interested.

Meetings or sales presentations without interaction between the client and the sales person are monologues without direction or purpose. They are usually a waste of everyone's time.

If there is no need or interest, there is no reason to present your offerings.

## 3)The final Close

People who feel that the customer will automatically place the order without being asked; are doomed to mediocrity or failure.

In most cases; even when making a great presentation, there will still be a need for a closing question to complete the mission.

### Prospects Expect you to Ask

The fact is that most clients expect a close at the end of any presentation. If there is no closing request, they are usually surprised and perhaps happy there is no commitment requested.

Some people starting out in sales expect that an order automatically comes after a good presentation, and they do not know any closes. Some will know two or three closes and feel prepared.

The truth is that most sales are made on the fourth or fifth attempt to close. Some may even take six or more. If a person knows only two or three closes, how successful do you think they will be?

# ESTABLISHMENT OF NEEDS

As Previously mentioned, the mistake often made by many salespeople is that they fail to qualify their prospect and establish if they have any needs or desire to consider a change.

They waste their own time, their company's time and their client's time by delaying the first part of the closing process which is to ***"qualify the prospect."***

## The Fear of a "NO"

Often it is just the fear of hearing a *"NO"* that holds the sales person back from qualifying their prospect. Many sales people feel secure in having many prospects who have not yet said either yes or no.

Surrounding oneself with many *Maybes* is dangerous because it creates a false comfort zone. Unfortunately, these comfortable salespeople do not realize that getting a NO is good, because it allows them to move on to the yes responses.

The removal of the No's allows the sales person to concentrate totally on the real potential.

Too often the salesperson does not qualify. They oversell themselves and their company and the appointments are made. The presentation is given to someone who has absolutely no need for their offerings and no desire to purchase them.

Why are we placing so much emphasis on this? The reason is that sales people keep making this mistake repeatedly. Perhaps they feel they are giving up too soon and the prospect needs convincing.

**Yes; Success can be a NO**

Success in prospecting does not always mean an appointment is made.

**A Positive Result can be a:**

- No - No need - Not interested - No desire to change

Yes, your list of potential clients may drop significantly; but, you now have more time to spend with your qualified prospects.

**Eliminating the No's** should be viewed as a huge success. When you treat a No as a positive thing, you will not fear one. You will then able to concentrate on the people with the real potential to buy your offerings.

**They are the ones with the yes.**

**You just say to yourself** *"That's great another NO out of the way, I am now getting closer to the Yes's."*

**The yes prospects will eventually say:** *"YES I will purchase your offerings*

***"If you do things right"***

### Qualifying a Prospect's Needs

This is the first part of your closing process; and like the early pioneering prospectors crouched over a river, it involves removing the debris, so you can get to the gold (the order).

**Do not fear the "NO" Responses**

**They are Necessary to get to the YES ones**

### Create a list of Qualifying Questions

Each type of offering (product or service) will have a few qualifying questions you can use. Make a list of as many simple questions that will qualify your prospect for a need or interest.

### Your Opening Remarks

Create a compelling introduction of yourself and your company. Do not babble on about nothing.

Quickly state the reason for your call in a manner that will get their attention and create interest and a desire to hear more.

Remember that you are not calling for your needs, you are looking for prospects who can benefit from your products or services. Once the interest has been created, do not waste time. Get right into your questions.

### Some Sample Questions for Industrial Sales

**You Ask** – "In your manufacturing process:

1. Do you paint your product or send it out to be painted?
2. Do you do any welding?
3. Do you exhaust any contaminants to atmosphere?
4. Do you use packaging materials?
5. What type of material handling equipment do you use?
6. What types of software do you use?

Let the client know that you are asking these questions to qualify if they could possibly benefit from your offerings before you make an appointment and waste both of your times.

You are not only showing respect for their time, you are showing that you are organized and thorough in your efforts to help your clients. You are not available unless there is some interest and a reason for a visit.

Structure your questions and information provided; so that the reason for your appointment, is very clear to your prospect. This method of Qualification will eliminate most of your wasted calls where there is no need or interest.

It is better to quickly eliminate 10 prospects with no need or interest through these questions, rather than make 10 appointments and waste gas, and perhaps 2 – 3 days doing the qualifying in person.

Prospects will often be surprised if they need to qualify for a visit. You should phrase it so that it appears to be respect for their time.

## Finding More Needs

Needs will take many forms and can be as simple as supplying a product or service. It could be a more involved process which may require finding the solution to a complex problem.

It might be price related or quality, service, size and maybe even appearance. Each type of direct sales will have its own requirements.

You should develop a complete inventory of ways in which your offerings can satisfy your prospects interests – whatever they may be. Your offerings will determine the questions that you will ask.

Each type of direct sales will involve different questions and different client needs. It will be your job to find the right qualifying questions for the type of direct sales company that you represent.

**You will then guide the prospect through the complete process**

Here are just a few examples of needs that you might look for. They all can become trial closes to qualify your prospect when you ask if they want to achieve something.

**The Questions below can relate to many client types**

**You Ask** – Would you like to:

- Save energy?
- Reduce labor costs?
- Increase quality?
- Reduce noise?
- Remove odors, smoke or harmful particulates?
- Solve a safety infringement?
- Reduce water consumption?
- Reduce your down time, or Increase Production Efficiency?
- Save on process material costs?
- Reduce floor space?
- Replace old equipment with better technology?
- Improve service response time?
- Cut costs of office products, or shipping costs and time?

**Each yes** to one of these questions about needs, will become a key point in your introductory meeting and your final presentation.

## Willingness to Change

Along with establishing a need, you will be faced with the prospects willingness to make a change.

There is no sense in proceeding if the prospect is absolutely opposed to making any changes to their present suppliers. Make the effort however, as most purchasers will resist change and object to your effort. It is a normal reaction.

**Not Interested in a visit**

You can send them some information for them to look at, and then move on. Follow up at a future time to see if you sparked some interest.

**Goal Met**

If you can establish a need, show the benefits and create a willingness to listen further; you have completed the initial qualifying of your prospect.

The qualifying questions or small mini-closes you use while establishing needs, should not be intimidating, because they show the client that you are working with them to meet their requirements or solve a problem.

Before you can build confidence and trust, you must become a comrade in arms with your prospect.

You must take whatever time and effort is required to provide them with the right answers and proper solutions.

### Keep on Track

Along the way, you should be constantly reaffirming that your prospect is happy with your progress and that you are on the right track.

These are the qualifying closes or questions; and if done correctly, they will seem like part of finding the perfect solution for the prospect.

At the end of your presentations when you have put in all the effort to satisfy your prospects requirements; and have shown the benefits of your offerings, you should still be asking for the order not waiting for it to arrive.

**The Final Close** is where you will find out if you have covered all the bases and met or solved all their requirements.

# ABOUT CLOSING

Closing questions are used everywhere in life; but in sales, they are very important tools that you will use to succeed.

They are not wrong because they will help you achieve the results that the company wanted when they hired you.

**Or the Results You Wanted**

**When you Started your Business**

The closes will help you reach all your sales targets and achieve your personal financial goals as well. Why spend all the time and money to reach the end of the selling process, if you do not ask for the sale.

Most prospects expect you to close because it gives them the chance to say no, ask a question or a chance to say yes.

**Without Closing**

**You have No Destination**

The final close or request for a purchase order is where every presentation is headed and everyone, especially your prospect, knows it.

**Do not Disappoint them!**

If you do not ask, you may not get the sale. You could deprive the prospect from saying yes to the close which you have omitted from your presentation.

The fatal mistake that is most often made by many sales people, is that they know only one close or will make only one attempt to close.

When the prospect says no, the sales person may be faced with an objection or question and will try and handle it.

If that does not work; they are defeated, and to go but back to the office or home. This is especially true, if they know only one close.

## How many times do you need to close?

The reality is that most sales are made on the fourth or fifth closing attempt; so, if you only know two or three closes, you have already limited your chances for success.

**Like a Person Fishing**

If one starts fishing and they have only one lure to use, the fish may not find it persuasive enough to go after, or it could get snagged on the bottom and the fishing is over.

**The Day is Lost**

## The Secret

The secret to successful closing is to learn as many different closes as you can find. Once learned, practice them until the wording is you; and does not sound like someone else's words, that you are reciting.

Each close will suit a different set of circumstances and you will eventually see the signs of when and where to use the right one.

Learn the closes; understand how and why they work so you can put them into your own words. They will then become as natural as breathing.

They will then not be intimidating or appear to be pressure tactics to your prospects. The entire prospecting and presentation process is a close. As we said earlier, the minute you open your mouth, you start the close.

**The Best way to Learn**

**When it is time to Make your Final Close**

**Is by Closing Too Soon and Too Often**

By asking closing questions or qualifying your prospect frequently, you will rarely appear to be applying pressure. You are simply doing things correctly to look after your prospect's best interests.

## Closes Generate Objections

Expect Objections as they are part of the process. You will soon learn in the next part of the training, that Objections are good things. They are clues that can show a prospects weakness or their reason to buy.

If you are not getting objections you are probably not asking enough qualifying or closing questions.

Many prospects will have a few pet objections that they know will stop most sales people in their tracks when they start to ask for the order.

Arm yourself with as many closes and answers to objections as you can. All you need is one more closing question or answer to their objection; than the prospect can present, and you win the prize.

## Closes and Answering Objections are a Team

They are the dynamic duo of successful selling. When you have mastered the closes and learned how to answer objections (which we also call questions) you will be in control of your own sales destiny.

We will be providing eleven main closing methods plus many smaller closing questions for you to get started with. *(Overcoming Sales Objections will be Part 3)*

There are many more closing methods than the ones we will outline here in this part of our training. If you are serious about sales, you will keep reading, listening and learning new closes.

## You will Never know too many

The more closes and answers to objections that you learn and commit to memory, that become part of your tool kit in sales; the higher will be your closing ratio and earnings.

Make sure you have covered everything necessary in your presentation and you feel that there is nothing left for you to say or add. Then you ask the Final Closing Question to Purchase your products or services.

# THE GREATEST CLOSING TIP EVER!

**THE MOST IMPORTANT PART TO**

**CLOSING**

**IS**

**Whenever you Ask a Closing Question**

---

## SHUT UP!!

## SHUT UP AND LISTEN!!

**After you have asked a closing question**
**The First person that Speaks**

## LOSES!!

---

I do not know what happens to sales people. They ask a closing question and they wait a few seconds, they get excited and they panic.

They then start babbling on and try to add more to their presentation.

---

## WHAT HAPPENS?

**They let their Prospect "Off the Hook."**

**AND YOU KNOW WHAT ELSE HAPPENS?**

## THE SALES PERSON LOSES!!!

**There is no Greater Pressure to a Closing Question than**

***"THE SILENCE"***

**That comes after it…. So**

**SHUT UP AND LISTEN!**

**The Prospect will either give you**

An Important Answer

An Order...Or

They will have an Objection (question)

After the next part of our training, you will be able to handle the objections as well.

**An Objection** is a reason for hesitation or a question that needs to be answered before you can complete the sale.

**Without Qualifying and Closing Questions**

**You would Never reach the point**

**Where you get an Objection.**

## What Closes Accomplish

- Mini closes provide you with answers and confirmations along the way.
- Knowing your Closes provides you with a place to go, after you have completed your presentation.
- Your Main Closes will either get the order or raise an objection.
- Raising the Objection provides the means to confirm the sale is yours.

Closes are the means to achieve your goals in this entire process of sales. They are not called closes without reason as they provide closure to all the events leading up to and including getting the sale.

There is no better feeling of confidence or control, then knowing how to get the sale when you are at the end of your journey.

**Closing Creates the Prospects Moment of Decision**

**Answering Objections is the other half**

**Of the Dynamic Duo Team**

**To Solidify the Order**

# CLOSING QUESTIONS

## What are Closing Questions

As we have already said, one way of making your closing ratios higher, is to ask small closing questions throughout all your meetings with your clients.

These questions are also indicators to show if you still have a real prospect and continue to have their interest.

If you do not have a real prospect or their interest, you will not only need to know it; but, you will need to dig deeper, try harder or look elsewhere.

There is nothing worse than allowing someone to listen to your entire presentation without finding out if they are a real candidate for your offerings.

Closing Questions will help you to prevent wasting time when no sale is there.

**They are Your Directional Tools**

**They are the**

1. What?
2. When?
3. Where?
4. Why?
5. How?
6. Which?

Methods for you to get an order, or the way to eliminate a no need or no desire. Closing Questions are the shortest forms of closing that will cause your prospects to purchase from you.

## Ways to Ask Closing Questions

### The Indicators

Whenever you ask a question that begins with a verb, the answer is always either a yes or a no indication revealing a person's preference. The person who is asking the question(s) has control.

**Sample Indicating Questions starting with a verb**

1. Do you prefer the red or the yellow enclosure?
2. Will you be happy with fewer rejects?
3. Is your main goal to increase productivity?

**There are also two types of questions**

1. Open ended Questions
2. Closing Questions

## 1) The Open-Ended Question

Open ended questions are used to get the prospect to explain their thoughts or concerns in more detail.

These questions will be used in your exploration of where or why they might need your offerings.

You may also want to have more information to solve a problem, meet a need or show a benefit.

**Sample Open-ended Questions**

- What quality problems are you having?
- How much time are you trying to save?
- Where are your production bottlenecks?
- Why are you changing the plant location of your packaging?

## 2) Closing Questions

The closing question directs the client to a yes or a no and moves them in the direction of a sale.

When you ask these types of questions, you already have the information you need and are in the process of securing the order.

**There are two types of Closing Questions**

1. Positive.
2. Negative.

### 1) Positive Closing Questions

If the positive question gets a YES; (this is what you are after in this approach). It moves you towards a sale.

If you get a no from these questions, change directions to get them back into the "Yes" mode.

**Examples:**

- Are you using this type of product in your production?
- Is this what you are looking for?
- Will you be deciding this week?

If the positive closing question gets a NO, it can be considered as directional or an elimination process and you need to keep going until you start getting yes answers again.

### 2) Negative Closing Questions

If the negative question gets a NO (This is what you are hoping for), and it moves you towards a sale.

**Here a NO response Is**

**A positive Directional Indicator for you**

Getting a yes to a negative close is **NOT** a good response and **NOT** what you are after.

**Examples of Negative Closing Questions:**

- Are you happy with your present supplier?
- Is their product providing all the benefits you need?
- Are you happy with the delivery times of your present supplier?
- Are you happy with the quality of your present supplier's product?

If the negative question gets a YES, you need to continue until you start getting NO answers.

## Final Closing Questions

When we use Final Closing Questions we are looking for confirmation of the order. Many times, all we need to use is this simple form of closing to get the sale.

The client has shown all the buying signals and the time is right for a simple question, the answer to which, confirms they have bought.

### Closing Question Tips

Many times, you need only to ask for the order in a simple question.

- It could be at the end of your presentation.
- It could be after using one or more of your closing methods and you need a simple confirmation that they have bought.
- It could be after answering an objection or many objections (questions); you also need clarification and confirmation.
- You need to know if you have met their concerns and if they are now ready to proceed.

**Often it is all that you Need**

**To get the order**

## Twelve Sample Final Closing Questions

1. Can we consider this is a yes for our product/service/project?
2. Shall we start by initialing the changes on the proposal?
3. Do you have a Purchase Order number?
4. Will you be proceeding with the order now that we agree?
5. Are you ready to get started with the project/service?
6. IF we have completely answered all your concerns, shall we get started with the order?
7. Does this mean that we are now your supplier of this product/service?
8. Have we now met all your needs to supply our offerings?
9. Shall we now consider that we are proceeding with the project?
10. When can we schedule the first shipment?
11. When would you like us to start the service?
12. When would you like the drawings for approval?

There are many more that you will be able to create for your offerings. Start a list of simple questions and keep adding to it. It is often these simple closing questions that will unlock the stalled ordering process and clarify that they have bought.

**These Smaller Closing Questions can:**

- Eliminate the need for a larger closing method
- Assist you when clarification of an order is needed

# INTRODUCTION TO THE CLOSES

## YOUR FIRST ELEVEN CLOSES

These should become some of the closes that you will use in many areas along the way to get the order. They can be used anywhere and not just at the end when you are asking for final confirmation of the purchase.

Each one will have a distinct time when its use will become obvious to you. With experience, you will clearly recognize when, where and why to use a one.

### Your Destinations

These closes are the ports where you are headed on your sales journey. Some will be used part way through the journey and others will become closes that you will use when you reach your destination.

By knowing them you can also create many new variations and shorter or longer ones to suit a situation.

Knowing these closes will provide confidence and power. You will know that your journey is not without the means of closure. You will know that when you get to the end of your final presentation that you have control over the outcome to get an order.

### Do not stop at 11 closes

As we have said earlier these are just eleven of the basic closes that are available. They will give you the opportunity to handle most situations that you will encounter.

It will take the use of four or five of these closes in many selling situations to get the order. Do not be afraid to use as many as it takes.

Closes are the vehicles you will use to provide a positive outcome during your journey; and obtain the success you desire, at the end of your journey.

## Close # 1 - Alternate of Choice

This alternative of choice close is one that is used everywhere.

**It is used:**

- When making appointments - choosing the time, day or week
- As minor closes in the presentation
- In the final closing of the sale itself

**How and Why it works**

If you give your prospect only one choice; the answer will more often be a NO, than a yes.

People like choices and when you ask the question: "Which do you prefer?" They feel that they are in control.

They may not choose either; but, they will probably tell you what they prefer as an alternative.

**Examples:**

**Setting the Week and Day of an Appointment**

1. *"Would you prefer next week or the following week?"*
2. *"Is Monday good or is Wednesday a better day next week?"*

**Setting the time of day is next**

1. *"Which is best for you, mornings or afternoons?"*
2. *Afternoons great*
3. *"Would 1:30 PM be OK or would 3:00 PM be a better time for you?"*

**Confirm the appointment when you are done**: *"OK we will see you next week on Wednesday at 1:30.*

It is a comfortable way of controlling and directing the time that you will see your client.

In most cases the prospect is not intimidated by these types of questions as they are normal and used by most, when setting appointments.

## Sample Alternate of Choice Qualifying/Closing

### a) General Questioning

- *Which is most important for you - price or quality?*
- *Do you have a preference of – North American made products or will off shore be acceptable?*
- *Do you prefer - Contractual services or do you order on an "as required" basis?*

### b) During your Information Gathering

- *Was it less space or less noise that was most important?*
- *Which model do you prefer, the C100 model or the C150 with extra outlets?*
- *What is the maximum part length, six feet or ten feet?*
- *Do you prefer the mounted unit, or the portable type?*

### During Final Presentation

- *Which layout do you prefer, number one, or number two?*
- *Which color would you like, the yellow or the blue?*
- *Would May 1st be a good start date, or would you prefer May 15th?*

As a final close, make sure the client has enough information, as this is a simple question and requires only a simple answer.

## Close # 2 - Order Blank

This is perhaps the most basic close of them all and will consist of a simple request to obtain your prospect's signature of approval.

Before presenting any document for approval, one must be sure they are showing exactly what the customer wants or has verbally agreed to, or it will not work.

You mast review its contents with your client completely and ask your mini-closes during this process. When you are finished and there are no issues, ask them to - *OK it or approve it.*

**NEVER ASK THEM TO SIGN IT!!**

### For Your First Order

It could come after introducing and testing your offerings and you have made an initial list of requirements to start the delivery of your products.

**Note:** This will not work as an easy close if you have not dealt with all their requirements or if they still have unanswered concerns.

### Move Slowly

If you rush this close before it makes sense to use it, you may be starting over from the beginning.

You should have already obtained a few yes responses or indications that they agree.

You might need to use more than one of these to get the final go ahead.

- *Is there any reason why we cannot proceed?*
- *Do you have any concerns to prevent us from getting started?*
- *Shall we get things underway?*
- *What Purchase Order Number shall I use for reference?*

At the appropriate time. you can turn the paperwork around and hand the prospect your pen and ask them to approve it or OK it.

### For Repeat Business

This is often used after you have established a working relationship with a prospect, and you are there to get an order.

You will use this when you have just completed a final review of their inventory or presented a list of your recommendations. You simply show them your list and ask them to OK it?

### A Larger Order

It could also be used at the end of a 20-page presentation that has been given by you.

You have several hard copies that outline all the criteria that the customer has asked for, and you have answered all the questions.

If required; you should have made the changes to the proposal as you have gone through it, you have initialed each change and each page as you proceeded through the document.

You should wait until the entire proposal has been reviewed and you have made all the changes and placed your initials beside the changes.

You now placc your signaturc in thc appropriatc location on the final page of the proposal and date it.

**You then turn the proposal toward the client and you ask the following:** *"Let's review the changes we have made and if you agree with the wording of the change, just place your initials beside mine."*

When all changes have been initialed they may automatically put their signature on the document and date it as you have done.

**If they hesitate, you simply say:** "All that's left is for you to approve the document, date it and we can get started."

### If Requested

At this point the customer may not like the idea of the initialed document.

You can indicate that after they have initialed the changes; and approved and dated all the copies; you will prepare a new clean document.

By initialing and approving this one, you can use your copy to create a clean copy for each of you.

They will retain their copy of the initialed one until the new one is completed and be able to verify all the changes have been made correctly.

**Note:** The new clean copy may be a necessary step, but it should not prevent you from getting an order with the initialed one.

If there have been many changes, additional descriptive wording has been added and initialed and the document is cluttered, it may simply be a comfort thing.

By initialing and approving the altered document before you leave, you have achieved a sale.

## The Right Way to Ask

- Do not - ask them to Sign it.
- To sign you need a lawyer.
- Ask them to Initial the changes or OK it or APPROVE it.
- Do not refer to it as a Contract!
- The same situation exists regarding needing a lawyer.
- Refer to it as a document or an Agreement.
- People will OK or Approve a document or an Agreement.
- They just won't Sign a Contract.

Always provide the new clean copy initialed and signed. Provide several copies of your initialed and approved clean document with the client.

Ask if they want to review it now or shall you come back tomorrow or the next day to pick up your copy. Do not panic if they want to look it over. You have the original hand written one and it is a legal commitment.

## Close # 3 - Question/Question

The question/question situation is one of the most obvious of all the buying signals that exists, yet sales people are almost always missing this opportunity to close.

The client's question usually comes from a position of real interest in the product or service. The prospect is ready to buy and has a simple question.

This is where many sales people miss their chance to close.

Without thinking or recognizing the opportunity or the buying signal, the sales person simply answers the question and misses the opportunity to get the order.

**YOU MUST!**

**Answer their Question**

**With Your Question**

### 1. Sample question by Prospect - Start Date

**The prospect asks:** *"Can you start in two weeks?"*

**Here is the Wrong way to Answer**

**The Unprepared sales person says**: *"Yes we can"*.

Why was this just answered the wrong way?

Yes! It is a correct answer,

But the wrong one for closing

They just lost an opportunity to close.

This simple response has just left the closing process open ended and will require more closing attempts.

**Answered the right way**

**Reply to it with a Question in this way:** *"If we can start in two weeks, shall I schedule it for then?"*

Now – when the client says YES

They have made the purchase

It is so simple, that it is often not recognized.

## 2. Sample question by Prospect - Colour

**The prospect asks:** *"Can I get it in Blue?"*

**The sales person replies:** *"Yes you can get it in Blue."*

**The Wrong way to answer again!**

Why have they just answered the wrong way?
Again, it is a correct answer
But the wrong one for closing
And they missed the sale.

**Answered the right way**

**Answer the Question with a Question:** *"Do you want it in Blue?"*

If they say YES!
The prospect has bought.

## 3. Sample question by Prospect - Model Type

**The prospect asks:** *"Does it come as a portable unit?*

**Another Wrong way to Answer**

**The sales person says:** *"Yes!"*

Again, answered the wrong way
Again, a correct answer
But the wrong one for closing
It is not going to get the sale

**Answered the right way**

**Answer the question with a question:** *"Do you want the portable unit?"*

When the prospect says YES,
They have bought.

Do not just answer yes!
Turn their Question into your Closing Question
And
**GET THE ORDER!**

## Close #4 - Free Trials

We will outline two approaches for **Free Trials** - A, and B. We will show the trial parameters of each.

We will summarize and provide the closing method which will be similar for approaches A and B, because they are trials using tangible offerings.

### Approach A) Free Trial - No Up Front Close

**The Trial Parameters**

This approach is often used with offerings that will involve a larger cost for equipment or services.

It could also involve a significant change in the present way of how the client is doing things.

The product or service may be a new concept or just new to the client.

The prospect is uncertain of the benefits or its dependability or Return on Investment. They are reluctant to try something different or new.

The prospect is probably satisfied with their existing equipment, products or services and needs a nudge to consider something else.

**What better way than a "Free Trial"**

This is a soft sell approach that gives the sales person the opportunity to get a foot in the door. (as the saying goes)

Their prospect can try something at no cost or up-front commitment, which often eliminates any objections.

It is an extremely good way to introduce products or services that perform better, increase productivity, are easier to use, reduce cost of materials, increase quality or improve appearance.

**In the end**

**The Product or Service Sells Itself**

**Note:** In the following two examples, you will see how the trial is presented. You will change the wording to suit your own offerings.

There will be many versions because of the wide range of products or services that can be offered. The two examples are conceptual.

**Example 1 – Try the Offering for a set time for Free**

This is great for equipment or services that can be easily integrated into present activity. It can be used in both office or plant environments.

**This approach was used** a lot when ***Color TV*** first appeared. It is often referred to as the "Puppy Dog Close." The TV appliance dealer would approach the prospect in the store, who was looking at the color TV.

**The dealer would say:** *"I bet you are wondering if you could live with one of those things in your home."*

The customer was expecting the owner to try and sell it, and they did not. The sales person just asked an opening question. The relieved prospect probably breathed a sigh of relief.

**The prospect might say something like:** *"Yea I was sort of thinking that way."*

**The prospect is still expecting an attempt to sell.**

**Instead the store clerk would say something like this:** *"Why don't you try it out for a week?"*

*"We will deliver it and you can try it at no charge."*

*"If you find you cannot live with it, we will also come and pick it up at "no charge?"*

**The store owner knew the color TV would sell itself.**

On the next day after delivery, the store owner would simply call the prospect

**They would ask:** *"Do you have any questions on how to adjust the color or picture?"*

If there were questions, the owner answered them and then simply said "Enjoy" and would hang up.

**Again, there was no close, no pressure**

After having it for 4 – 5 days – the prospects wife loved it, his kids loved it, and all the neighbor's kids have been in to watch. Can he now say I do not want it?

Most of the time the prospect would call the store and ask: "How do I go about getting one of these things anyway?"

**Example 2**

It's the same close that car dealers have been using for years. The presentation has gone reasonably well but there is still some hesitation.

**The dealer says:** *"Why don't you take it for a test drive and see what it feels like behind the wheel."*

**When the prospect gets back**

**The Free Trial close has won again.**

**Some Examples of Free Trial Equipment**

a) Photocopy Equipment

b) Accounting Software

c) Material handling equipment: lift trucks, hand trucks

d) Process equipment: Paint Spraying systems, hand tools

## Approach B) Free Samples - Free to use (no return required)

Often a company will allow their sales people to leave their prospects with free product samples for testing to see if they will meet the client's needs.

**No return or purchase is required**

This will usually be for consumables that are used in larger quantities.

There is not a lot of cost involved in the sampling process, when considering the size of the order at hand. Usually the volumes are large enough to easily write off the samples or products that are consumed.

## Setting the Parameters

**If you can use this method**; be sure you have explained or demonstrated the use of your offerings, so they can be tested properly.

**You Say:** *"There is only one way that you will know if our offerings:*

*Will do what I say"*

*Will increase office efficiency"*

*Will work in your plant"*

*Will improve production"*

*Will improve quality"*

*Will improve appearance:*

If they do not live up to the requirements, we have our answer and I will be on my way. If they do what I am saying, then you will have an alternative source for your needs.

### Some Examples of Free Trial Consumables

- Office supplies: copy paper, toner, coffee, floor mats
- Process Consumables: Sandpaper, cleaning chemicals, gloves
- Packaging supplies: sealing tape, boxes, plastic wrap

These items will usually be used in high enough volumes to justify a free trial.

## Trial Process for Approaches A and B

### Start the Trial

Make sure you have provided complete instructions for use and where required provided an actual demonstration. Before leaving, confirm that you have answered all their immediate questions.

Tell them you will call the next day to see if they have any further questions or need more instructions. You will then make or confirm your next appointment for after the trial, while you are there.

**You say:** "*When the trial is over, I will be looking for your comments on the outcome of the trial."*

*Your opinions are very important and are very much appreciated because I get to learn firsthand how people feel about the product." especially if they did not work out."*

### Feedback Statement

If you do not set this review and feedback requirement in place, they may feel that they have no need to see you.

You might find your equipment or any leftover products waiting for you at reception, when the trial is over.

### Call the next day after the Trial Start

Call to see if they have any questions about the use of the product or service. Do not leave it longer than one day to call in case there are questions, or your offerings may end up not being tested at all.

If they do have any questions, answer them and hang up. At this point, do not even ask if they like it so far!

**If they did not say:** *"Your offerings did not work out, come and get your equipment or samples we have left"*

**Consider the telephone call**

**A preliminary close and a positive response**

### Re-Start of a Trial

If the prospect asks a question or two, answer them. If there are too many questions about the equipment or service or they have used your samples and are asking for more, suggest getting together.

When you visit, they might expect an attempt to get an order even though you are just there to answer questions provide further instructions of use or provide more samples for testing.

This will allow you to get the trial re-started on a positive note and if appropriate, you can try a few qualifying mini closes while you are there. It is however, not the right time to ask for the order.

## The Appointment after the Trial

### The Normal Outcome

When you arrive, ask the person doing the assessment how it went. Answer any questions. They know why you offered the free trial and why you are there.

If the trial was successful, the prospect will either order immediately, or they will expect you to ask for the order.

Now, you might use any of your closing options. The prospect will either come up with an objection or purchase it.

### Possible Roadblocks

You could arrive for your appointment and your equipment or leftover samples are at reception for you to pick up. They may be trying to just return your offerings without seeing you.

If this is the case, ask to see them when you are there so you can learn why things did not work out. If that is not possible, try to make a follow up appointment.

For some people, this *"no access"* is their easy way out and saying no.  They will not be faced with your request to purchase and you do have their answer.

**If this is the case**

**Leave it for a Future call back**

**and Move On**

## Close # 5. - The Comparative List (Ben Franklin)

### When to Use this Close

You have made your presentation and the customer's needs have been met. Quotes have been presented and price is not an issue.

The customer is interested and has said they want your product or service but cannot decide whether it is the right time to proceed or not.

At this point; for the prospect, there appears to be no urgency and there is no indication that they wish to move forward with an order now.

The prospect is hesitating, unable to decide, and you may have already made one or two other closing attempts, without success.

**They may be saying:** *"I just don't know if it's the right time."*

It is now your job to move them from this position of indecision, to one of moving forward by placing the order.

**Yes - They Are Procrastinating!**

They have said that you will be the supplier. It appears that it is not a question of who will be getting the order when it is placed.

**Their Question is When**

**Or a little bit If**

**They should Purchase it?**

### The Obstacles

- Using this with an experienced purchasing agent is not easy
- It has been around a long time
- Few buyers will allow you to do it
- Still try it if the situation fits

**Most often** it is used in a situation where the client is not a professional purchaser and is not used to making these types of buying decisions.

It could be a small business owner purchasing software, advertising or new office equipment.

It could be a homeowner purchasing a car, a new home, home renovations, life insurance or a cottage.

**This close is a tough one** but it works very well in the right circumstances. Experience will tell you if it is right.

**If you Proceed**, do not just jump right into this close. Prepare the client slowly and sympathize with them.

**You can say:** *"You know that you are not alone. Many people have found themselves in a similar position as you find yourself today."*

*"It is not often that you are making this kind of decision. It's not easy and I understand."*

**Pause for a second - And as if an afterthought**

**You say:** *"As a matter of fact there is a way that many people use to handle such a situation."*

**Optional** *"It is a method that many people including a former US President Ben Franklin used when he needed to handle tough decisions."*

*"Let's see if it might work for you? It is called the Ben Franklin Decision Process"*

**You add** – *"We will stop at any point if you wish."*

If they agree, you take out a piece of paper and draw a vertical line down the middle from top to bottom.

Then draw a horizontal line a little down from the top crossing the other line and creating a "t"

**Continue** - *" Here is what we will do. On one side of this page we will list the reasons why you should do it today, and on the other side we will list the reasons why you should not."*

*"Does that seem OK?"*

**If you get a Yes**

**You say:** *"I will start writing all of the reasons why it makes sense to move in a Positive direction today?"*

**Make sure you come up with a lot of reasons**

**You now ask:**

- "How about this?" - Provide the reason and write it down.

- "Is this a good reason?" - Write it down.
- "Does this make sense?" - Write it down.
- Keep asking and keep writing.

Make the YES list as-long-as you can

Finish the YES list first before you start the NO side

**Your Sample List**

| YES, Side | NO Side |
|---|---|
| Reason 1 – write it down | * Reason 1 help them |
| Reason 2 - write it down | * Reason 2 help them |
| Reason 3 - write it down | * Reason 3 stop here and let them do it |
| Reason 4 - write it down | * Reason 4 by them |
| Reason 5 – write it down | * Reason 5 by them |
| Reason 6 – write it down | * Reason 6 by them |
| Reason 7 - write it down | * Reason 7 by them |

We used the word POSITIVE when asking them to proceed.

We used the word NEGATIVE when we talk about not proceeding.

**When you are done the Yes Side**

**You say:** *"Let's think of all the Negative reasons why you should NOT move forward today."*

The words "Negative and Not" create a subtle way of indicating a wrong direction.

If the prospect has already mentioned several reasons why not to move forward with a purchase during your presentation, you write them down first and read them out loud as you write them.

**You then ask the question:** "*What else can we think of?*"

YOU HAND THEM THE PEN AND PAPER

**You say:** "It's your turn"

YOU THEN SHUT UP!

Your prospect will either start giving reasons and write them down, or they will give up.

**They might just say:** *"OK let's go ahead with the purchase."*

They might try to come up with more reasons not to do it today or they will end up presenting an objection. An Objection you will soon be able to handle.

If they come up with more reasons why not, you might be in trouble.

**A Usual Result**

Very often you get started with the YES reasons and they will feel foolish and say let's do it and you do not need to finish. This is very often the outcome to this close and why it is used successfully.

The prospect feels uncomfortable. It is almost like they are being treated as one might treat a child or pupil.

The positive reasons are so obvious that it becomes almost embarrassing and seems pointless not to proceed with the order.

**Summary of this Close**

We have referred to this close using Ben Franklin as the example. You may wish to ignore the reference to Ben Franklin altogether and that is your choice and OK.

**It's Origin**

It is what Ben Franklin used to do and it is where the name of the decision-making process came from. It has obviously been around for a long time.

**Note:** Never refer to it as a close when talking to the prospect. It is a "Decision Making Process" or "The Ben Franklin Decision Process"

**The Obvious Concept**

List the reasons for making a purchase (with a lot of help from you) and then leave them on their own to come up with the reasons why not to make the purchase.

**Yes, it can backfire and make the client angry**

**So, explain and ask permission first**

They could also come up with more reasons not to go ahead. That is why you need to present a lot of reasons why they should buy today.

It is entirely up to you if you wish to use it; so, find the most comfortable and professional way for you to present it.

**The Concept is There**

**And it Works!**

# SIMILAR SITUATIONS

## Overview

This close is very like the Ben Franklin Close and could often be used in its place for the same reasons. The main difference is that while the Ben Franklin close involves writing; this one is verbal.

### The Circumstances

You have already asked for the order and there seems to be uncertainty or just procrastination that is causing the client's hesitation.

Depending on your offerings the subject matter will differ; but, the concept of the close will be the same.

**We will outline two Alternative Closes**

**In which this can be Presented.**

The prospect has reacted favorably to your presentation and your offerings; but, they are reluctant to do something today. Again, they are uncertain if it is the right time or thing to do.

Many people will put off deciding even if it is the right one.

**You begin this close by saying:** *"I can understand how you feel."*

*(Short pause)*

**Continue** *"You know several (months, years) ago, our company called on a client who found themselves in a situation very like yours."*

*"They had the same questions and concerns that you are having right now, and this is what happened."*

**Right here** – You can go in one of two directions

- **Close #6 - The Positive Direction and Outcome**
- **Close #7 - The Negative Direction and Outcome**

## Close 6 - The Positive Direction and Outcome

Many people will put off deciding even if it is the right one.

**You begin this close by saying:** *"I can understand how you feel."*

*(Short pause)*

**Continue** *"You know several (months, years) ago, our company called on a client who found themselves in a situation very similar to yours."*

*"They had the same questions and concerns that you are having right now, and this is what happened."*

**The Positive Direction**

**You can say:** *"After we resolved their major concerns and ironed out all the details; like what we are doing here, they went ahead with the project."*

**Continue:** *"You know today they are enjoying higher profits, less rejects, higher quality, increased sales and happier clients"*

The list can go on for as long as you want to make it. It helps if you can have a name or testimonial letter available to show them.

Unless they are competitors in the same marketplace, you could even offer to let them talk to your client.

**Make sure Your Previous Client will allow this first**

**And, that they are Still Happy with the Results**

**You continue and say:** *"You know I feel good because we were able to show our client why they should move forward at that time, and now they are enjoying all of the benefits we have just talked about with you."*

*"I feel happy that we were able to help that company to become more profitable, more successful. That is what I would like to be able to do for you today.*

**The Preliminary Close:**

**You ask:** *"Would you be excited if the same results happened to your company in the next (six months, year)?"*

**If they say***:* *"YES"*

**You Say:** – *"So why don't we get started today?"*

**If they say no**

**or**

**If there is still hesitation**

**It is time for a recap**

**Your Recap**

**You Say:** *"We have reviewed your production methods, material costs, manpower and energy costs and you have already expressed your desire to:*

- *Expand your company*
- *Increase your profits*
- *Increase production*
- *Increase quality*
- *(Whatever it is)*

*"Is there any reason why you should stop your company from enjoying the benefits we have just outlined?*

**You are now at a Crossroads**

**If they say: *"No"***

**This is Good - You can now use a short closing question.**

**You Ask:** *"What was the delivery date you wanted, April or early May?"*

Keep going in this positive direction. Ask for a purchase order number or ask them to OK, APPROVE the document.

*If they say:* "YES, there is a reason

Not to get started."

Find out why and answer the objection and then try another close.

## Close #7 - Negative Direction and Outcome

It could be added after the Positive approach has failed. This is often referred to as the negative sales approach. Be careful!

**This one Could make a Prospect**

**VERY ANGRY!!**

**You say:** *"I can understand how you feel,"*

**(Short pause)**

**You Continue:** *"You know, several (months, years) ago our company called on a potential client who found themselves in a situation very like yours."*

*"They had the same concerns that you are having right now."*

*"Unfortunately, we were not successful in showing them why it was the right thing to do at that time."*

*"As a result, they were unable to improve production, and could not improve the quality or profitability.*

*Their sales continued to drop, and customers continued to leave, and now they realize they should have made the changes when they had the chance.*

**You Continue the close by using Result 1 or 2**

**Result 1** – They are in very bad shape, struggling to survive and can no longer afford to take full advantage of what we offered back then."

This could be difficult to provide a referral without breaching a trust.

**Result 2** – They are out of business"

**Do not use this unless it is true**

**You Say:** *"You know I feel bad because we were unable to show that client why it was right to move forward at that time. Had we done so, their position could have been so different than it is today."*

*"They would be enjoying the benefits the changes would have brought and now be a thriving business."*

**Back to their Situation**

**You Continue with** *"We have reviewed your production, material costs, manpower and energy costs and what this project will do for your company."*

*"Is there any reason why you should stop your company from enjoying the benefits we have outlined in our proposal?"*

**If their answer is a**

**"NO"**

**Continue with:** *"Let's get you started in that direction.*

**If it is a**

**"YES"**

It's on to more closes and Answers to Objections

**Summary**

There are unlimited ways to use this similar situation close. It means putting your client in someone else's shoes to visualize either a happy ending or bad one.

Each type of offering whether it is a product or service can be used to illustrate the outcome of making or not deciding to purchase.

**It is powerful, and it works**

## Close # 8 - Secondary Question

This close involves asking two questions in succession, with the second one being the easiest to answer.

When the second question is answered, they also will have answered the first, and confirmed that they have bought.

This one has also been around a long time and the approach should be very subtle. You will need to perfect this one before you try it as it may have the reverse affect as it may appear to be trickery.

**You will Know when this one is Right to use**

**When it is Used Incorrectly**

**It will be Called Trickery**

It is right when you have given and reviewed your entire proposal and they have agreed with the benefits and like the product or service you have offered.

Pricing has been reviewed and finalized and the terms and conditions have also been discussed and settled; but, they have not yet said the order is yours officially.

**You are Almost There**

You need to tip the scales just a little, and it needs just a little nudge to push them over the edge.

**This happens Sometimes**

**And it is Normal Occurrence**

Right now, the client is in a safe zone and is not committed and you need to get confirmation of the order.

**Make it Easier for them**

It makes it easier for them; because, when they say yes to a minor question, which is much easier to handle, it also means they have said yes to the major question.

**It works**

It sounds a little crazy, but some purchasers do not want to appear to be too easy to sell. This sort of gets them off the hook.

Make sure the secondary question is an easy one and you know what they will answer to start with.

**Do not Pause Between the Two Questions**

**1. A Correct Secondary Question Close**

**FIRST QUESTION** – *"It looks like we have reviewed everything and have answered all of your concerns. Have we reached an agreeable position for the project to be a go?"*

**DO NOT PAUSE!**

**SECONDARY QUESTION** – *"By the way would you want the delivery to be scheduled for June 15th or June 28th?"*

**When they Provide a Date**

**They have Bought**

**2. Another Correct Secondary Question Close**

**FIRST QUESTION** – *"We have outlined everything, and it appears that we have what you need, so shall we proceed now with the approvals of these documents?"*

**DO NOT PAUSE!**

**SECONDARY QUESTION** – *"By the way was that two copies you wanted for your records or three?"*

When they say the number of copies, they have bought

Even if they laugh at your closing method, it probably means they have bought. After their answer, use one of your short closing questions to confirm the order.

The worst thing that can happen is that you will get an objection.

**ANSWER THE OBJECTION**

**THEN TRY ANOTHER CLOSING QUESTION!**

There will be many secondary closes that relate to your product or service.

Make a list of possible secondary question combinations and make the list as large as you can.

**Memorize them and Use them**

## Close # 9 - Summary Question

This approach can be used to re-start stalled decisions and move the Prospect to a YES. It is also used after several failed attempts to close have occurred or maybe even more closing attempts were made.

**The client has not yet presented a clear objection**

Perhaps the prospect is confused, and does not want to decide, because something seems to be not-quite-right. At this point, they do not feel comfortable in moving forward until all doubt is removed.

Perhaps the prospect is not confused, and they are purposely avoiding making a final commitment.

They have not said no but they also have not said yes. You are stalled and need to get things moving again.

**This is not Uncommon**

You are there because at some point earlier, whether it was on your initial call, or during your fact-finding interview; that the prospect indicated they had a real interest in your product or service or demonstrated a definite need or problem to solve.

It has been re-affirmed during the final presentation, but something is still holding them back, and we need to find out what it is.

The summary question close is usually presented this way, because the prospect is stalled, and you cannot quite find out what they may be objecting to.

You have already made your entire presentation and they now act confused, or maybe even you are now confused.

**You now say:** *"Just to clarify my thinking,*

**Look Baffled or Confused**

**You Continue:** *"What part of our service/product/project is it that you find unclear and is causing you concern about moving forward today? "IS IT?"*

**DO NOT STOP!!!**

You immediately start going through the main points of your presentation and continue until you find the reason for their hesitation.

**You begin by asking:**

Is it this? (provide example)

Is it this? (provide example)

Is it this? (provide example)

**Continue asking until**

**They provide an Answer**

**If you stop after asking:** *"What part is unclear and keeping you from moving forward today?"*

**They will probably jump in and say:** "*The whole thing, I am just not sure.*

If that happens you are finished, or will have to start all over again, or find a way to get back to the Summary questions.

The important part here is to keep going and follow with a few questions of various things covered in your presentation.

1. *Is it the way we do this?*
2. *Is it this feature you are unsure of?*
3. *Is it this clause?*
4. *Is it that option?*

Use as many "is it's" as you can.

Keep going and cover the entire presentation if necessary OR until something is presented as the reason why they are hesitating.

**To Get to That Point**

**Summarize** the key points of your presentation. Make sure you cover the areas that you know may cause many people to hesitate.

At some point the prospect will probably identify the problem area:

**They may Say:** *"That's it! I feel uncomfortable about having so much down time during the project"*

**Then you say**: *"OH! - IS THAT IT?"* – (Look apologetic) *"I AM SORRY!! - Did I not cover that part well enough?*

**The following is the Five-Parts of Overcoming Objections**

Step1. QUESTION IT

Step 2. SHUT UP AND LISTEN to their entire explanation!

Step 3. CONFIRM THEIR ANSWER BACK TO THEM.

Step 4. ANSWER IT.

Step 5. CONFIRM YOUR ANSWER.

**Step 1. You Ask!** "Just what is it about the down time that has you concerned, or confused?"

**Step 2.** Hear them out! Shut up and Listen.

**Step 3. You now say:** *"So this is the area" (outline it) that was holding you back from moving forward today. Is, that right?"*

Look relieved that you have discovered the reason. Your client has now told you why they are hesitating.

**Continue with: "***If you were more comfortable with the amount of down time, it would provide you with the confidence you need to get started?" "Is, that right?"*

Or

*"If you understood how this part worked and saw that it did not interrupt your production time, and we could make the changes in non-production hours....*

*Would you feel more confident about getting started with the project?*

At this point the prospect has indicated that this is something that is holding them back from deciding today.

In the prospect's explanation, you have now learned why they are concerned.

**Step 4.** Answer how you will overcome this concern. If you answer all their concerns fully you should be able to ask for the order again.

**Step 5.** When you have fully covered the solution to the objection,

**You say:** *"So that completely answers that – Is that right?"*

**If your prospect says: "YES"**

**Use an appropriate short close to get the order.**

**If your prospect says**: *"NO"*

You can try another closing approach

PERHAPS TRY THE NEXT CLOSE

THE LOST SALE CLOSE

## Close # 10 - The Lost Sale

The lost sale close will use the very same ending as the Summary Close but it will start differently.

That is why it is called the LOST SALE.

BE CAREFUL! If you have already used the summary question close, and your presentation of the Lost Sale is too much like what you have already used, you might not get the order.

Or

You could even be escorted the rest of the way out of the building.

**The Approach**

When you have NOT been successful in any of your other closing attempts, you stop, close your books and look totally defeated.

You then stand up, thank them for their time and start moving towards the door so the prospect is convinced you are defeated and leaving.

**Here Comes the Switch.**

**You then stop. You turn and say**: *"I am sorry, that I was not good enough to show you that you should be proceeding today. Your response seemed to indicate you liked what you saw" (whatever has been presented)*

**You continue:** *"You know if I had been good enough, you could be looking forward to increased profits, increasing your quality, and improving your delivery service".*

**Use the things you talked about with them**

**Act very Upset and Concerned.**

**You continue on with the switch**: *"I am sure it was my poor explanation of our products/services that led to this moment?*

*"Just for my future presentations, and my own information, so that I do not make the same mistakes again; would you mind explaining just where I failed in my presentation.*

**Pause long enough for them to answer**

**Remember Shut up and Listen**

**If there is no help forthcoming**

**Start asking questions**

**Note:** Use completely different questions if you have already done a summary close.

> *"Did I fail to show you enough benefits?"*
>
> *"Did I fail show the complete versatility of our product?"*

Keep going until you get a reaction from your prospect.

**They might say:** *"I just do not see how your product will help us the way you say it will."*

**You ask:** *"Could you maybe explain why you feel this way?"*

**Shut up and listen to their Whole Answer**

**Repeat their Answer back to them**

**You say:** *"So that's it. I did not cover that well enough?"*

*"Before I leave, just so you have the right information, let's do a very quick re-cap and see if I can answer those areas for you."*

**Answer Their Concerns**

**Start a review saying**: *"You may remember this - you may remember this – we said this and keep going. Did I cover this? Did I tell you about this?"*

When you are sure you have covered their concerns completely,

**Confirm Your Answer**

**You can say:** *"That should answer your immediate concerns, have I missed anything?"*

> **If they say**: *"Yes,"*
>
> **Ask:** *"What did I miss?"*

**Carry on until they have nothing left**

**Whenever they say:** *"You have covered everything"*

**Finish with** *"Thank you for taking the time to explain where I went wrong (in not explaining the benefits well enough.")*

*"From your reaction, I can see you have more confidence in what we can do for you – Is that right?*

*"And it looks like we have hopefully answered all of your concerns – Is that right?*

## USE ANOTHER CLOSE

Probably a Short one will do

## Close # 11 - Closing on a Final Objection

The client has raised a few questions (objections) and you have addressed and answered them all.

You feel that your answers have created another chance to close the sale.

The prospect appears to have nothing left to throw at you, and you are still in their office. You must consider they are still interested, or still want your product or service.

**But, you are not Quite Sure**

The whole exercise has been somewhat confusing, and you are not sure if the last discussion was their final objection or not.

**You say:** *"You will admit that we have covered a lot of ground today, and it appears that we have answered all of your concerns. Is, that right?"*

**Your purpose here,** as a sales person, is to confirm that there are no more questions or objections.

**You continue**: *"Can you now think of any FINAL REASON(S) that would prevent us from moving forward with the order today?"*

**If they say:** *"NO"*

**You say:** "*That's great then I would say that means we have a go.*"

Or

**You say:** "*I would take that as a yes to our proposal.*"

**When they now say:** *"YES"*

It's time to finalize the order with a short closing question. You can ask them to approve the documents you have prepared or ask if they have a Purchase Order Number.

**CLOSE IT!**

# Time to Re-Group

## The Reason to Stop

The closes are designed to get orders or objections. Sometimes, despite everything you try, you cannot get an order.

It is very important to know when it is time to finally stop, and step back, before you push the client too far.

It is often a very difficult call

Sometimes you may not catch it in time

There is a thin line between Persistence and Annoyance

This may seem like it is giving up, but if you have made 7, 8 or even 10 closing attempts, and answered all the prospects objections, and you find them no longer receptive.

- Maybe they are even getting angry with you.
- They may even be showing their anger.
- This is not how you want to finish all your efforts.
- If you wear out your welcome completely you will not get back in.

**Stop Before it is too late, if you can!**

We know that often pushing the client to the annoyance level gets an order.

**But this time it's Different**

You can see you will not get the order today. It's time to step back and salvage the situation, so you can possibly have a chance to come back again.

**You might say:** *"I respect your position and I see you are not ready to make a decision today."*

**You Continue:** *" I AM LEAVING because the most important thing here is for you to feel comfortable about placing the order when you are ready."*

*"It is apparent that today, right now is not the right time. - Am I right?"*

**They will probably say**: *"Yes that is definitely Right"*

**You Continue:** *"You know I have been trying very hard to get an order here, and that's my job."*

*"I believe our product/service will provide everything you are looking for and I am truly sorry if I have pushed so hard."*

*"I hope we can see you again when you are ready?"*

**If they say yes, you ask:** *"When do you think that you might be ready to make that decision?" or "When might that be?"*

**Wait for the answer**

**And ask:** *"How do you see our chances?"*

**Wait for the answer and you finish by saying:** *"I will check back with you (name the date mentioned).*

**Perhaps Add the Following**

*"May I ask if you have any concerns with me, our company, our product or offerings?"*

*"Are there any changes that you would like to see or additional information you would like to have?"*

Write down everything indicated and repeat the list back to them.

**You then say:** *"Thank you for your time today and the information just provided.*

**You Continue:** *"I will do a total review of our proposal including the areas of concern that we just discussed. I will also see what other benefits I can add as well."*

*"I understand and respect your reasons for hesitation and will use this new information to provide something that you will be much happier with."*

If a time to call was given, confirm it again, before you leave.

**You Say:** *"I will call next Wednesday to arrange a time that is suitable for our revised proposal presentation."*

**If this new opportunity happens to you**

**Get Prepared**

**You Need to:**

- Review of all the events from your first contact until the end of your unsuccessful presentation.

- Find something that you can change or add; because, something new provides an additional reason to present your offerings again with these value-added items.
- Make sure you cover all the details and areas of interest that you have previously discussed.
- Provide solutions to all the concerns that were expressed on your last visit.
- Get any additional information that they have requested.
- Make all the changes they have requested.
- There will be answers somewhere in your failed attempt that will improve your future efforts.
- Look for them! Find all of them!

Call back at the discussed time to arrange a meeting.

**Do not ask for their Answer**

**That is often a Disaster**

**If you ask** "*Have you had enough time to think about it?*

**Their reply could very well be** "Yes we have, and the answer is No!

**And it is over**

**You should start by saying:** *"On my last visit there were a few things that were not quite right. We have made those changes and added some additional items and reviewed our pricing.*

*"What time is suitable for us to come in for a final review?" (Use your alternate of choice to arrange the meeting)*

When you get the appointment, you will be doing a

**CALL BACK**

# SUMMARY OF CLOSING THE SALE

Some people put off qualifying or asking for the order because:

- They are afraid the customer will say no or not interested
- They do not know enough closes.
- They do not know any or enough answers to objections.

It could be fear that they have not done a good enough job of presenting.

Because of these fears, they stall, and they dance around waiting for the prospect to say that they want to place an order.

While they play this waiting game, they end up not even asking for the order.

If this happens all their time and effort to date, could be totally lost.

**The Best approach**

1. Learn these closes and more.
2. Memorize them and rehearse them with Enthusiasm.
3. Learn your Answers to Objections. (Next)
4. Do not change the overall concept or intent of the closes.
5. Do make them part your own personality and find your unique way of presenting them.
6. If the timing is not right to get the order, the next best thing is to find out where you stand and request thc opportunity to come back.
7. If you know your closes and the answers to objections, you will be in control and will never need to fear a no or an objection.
8. Do not be Afraid to use your own Personality to Close
9. Never Avoid Making the actual Attempt to Close

**WHEN YOU ASK THE CLOSING QUESTION**

**SHUT UP**

**AND LISTEN!!!**

**The first person to speak**

**LOSES!**

Do not be afraid to use more than one close. Most sales occur on the fourth of fifth closing attempt. If you know only two or three you will miss many potential sales.

**The Benefits of this Skill Set**

- Qualifying and Closing gives you the opportunity to make sure you are working with a qualified prospect.
- You are also able to show them that your main objective is to help meet all their needs and provide solutions to any problem.
- This process will keep you on track and provide the feedback you need to confirm whether your efforts are successful.
- You know where you are headed with any meeting or presentation.
- You will know what to do when you finish your final presentation.
- You will know how to ask for the order.

# CLOSE IT!

***END OF PART TWO***



*Wayne E Shillum - Author*

www.ingramcontent.com/pod-product-compliance
Ingram Content Group UK Ltd.
Pitfield, Milton Keynes, MK11 3LW, UK
UKHW051129260726
13967UKWH00010B/2943